THE FRENCH IN AMERICA

THE **FRENCH** IN AMERICA

VIRGINIA BRAINARD KUNZ

Executive Secretary
Ramsey County Historical Society

Published by
Lerner Publications Company
Minneapolis, Minnesota

Third Printing 1968

Copyright © 1966 by Lerner Publications Company

Library of Congress Catalog Card Number: AC 66-10146

...CONTENTS...

Daniel Greysolon, Sieur du Luth, visited the head of Lake Superior and the Minnesota country in the 1670's. He worked out treaties with the warring Indian tribes to make the area safe for French fur traders. The city of Duluth, Minnesota, commemorates the name of this explorer.

PART I.

Trailblazers and Traders

1. *French Exploration for the Northwest Passage*

In December of 1523, 31 years after Columbus, an Italian sailing under the Spanish flag, had discovered America, another Italian set forth on a voyage of exploration. His name was Giovanni da Verrazano, and he sailed under the banner of Francis I, King of France. Francis, like the other rulers of his time, was eager to discover a passage through North America to the rich East Indies and Cathay. His orders to Da Verrazano were to find such a route.

Da Verrazano, with a crew of Frenchmen and a French captain, Antoine de Conflans, sailed from Dieppe, an important port in northern France on the English Channel. They headed down the Channel and out into the Atlantic at a time of year which does not offer the best of weather for seafaring, for the North Atlantic in winter is rough and stormy. So they sailed south to the Madeira Islands and then turned west to cross the great ocean.

Their ship, of course, was a sailing vessel, probably much like those used by Columbus — broad and deep with three or four masts, high sides and the bow and stern rising above the main deck.

By the middle of March, Da Verrazano had reached the North American coast, probably near the Carolinas. After sailing south for some distance ("fifty leagues," he wrote later in a report to King Francis), he turned about and sailed northward along the coast. He passed New York harbor and the mouth of the Hudson River, and reached Nova Scotia before returning to Dieppe the following July.

Even as early as 1524, France was lagging behind the other great nations of Europe in exploring that strange new mass of land lying in the western sea and blocking passage between the Old World and the Orient. Not only Spain, but Portugal and England, had sent out ships on voyages of exploration in the early years of the 1500s. France's own hardy fishermen had been fishing the waters off Newfoundland since about 1504.

But though France was tardy in arriving in the New World, and though she did not try to set up colonies for many years, the men she sent out to explore America were truly pathfinders and trail-blazers.

Today the map of the United States from the Great Lakes to the Gulf of Mexico and from the Appalachian Mountains to the Mississippi River is sprinkled with their names. They brought their language to the quiet forests and rushing streams and they left it upon the rivers they discovered, the forts and trading posts they set up, the towns they founded.

Explorers sent out by other countries touched the fringes of the North American continent, but the French were the first Europeans to plunge inland, to stand upon the soil of America's "heartland." They discovered the Mississippi River and the Great Lakes. They founded America's two largest cities, Chicago and New York.

These adventurous men of France began trading with the Indians for furs and their trade opened up the interior of the American continent. This vast new land was no longer a mysterious reach of dark forests and broad prairies. It became an inviting wilderness beckoning the later pioneers to settle there.

The influence of the French upon American life has always been far greater than the number of French men and women who came to America to live. The French actually did not come in great numbers. Some who came, such as the hundreds of French soldiers and sailors who fought beside the American Colonists during the American Revolution, did not stay at all but went home to France. Yet, the French have had an impact upon America which has been far out of proportion to their numbers here.

In the beginning, France and her kings were not interested in setting up colonies. Their chief concern was with finding a water route around or through this new continent, which was so inconveniently blocking their attempts to sail west to reach the East and China.

Jacques Cartier, the first French explorer to set foot in the New World. He claimed the soil of Canada for France.

In 1534, with 62 men and two small ships, Jacques Cartier set off on the first of three voyages. This daring French sailor probably had been with Da Verrazano on his voyage 10 years earlier. Under orders from King Francis I, he set his course for Newfoundland. Francis wished him to search not only for a Northwest Passage but also for new lands for France, and for gold and "other riches."

Cartier sailed into the Gulf of St. Lawrence and landed on the Gaspe Peninsula, near the mouth of the St. Lawrence River. Here he went ashore and claimed the land for France. He was back the next year and sailed up the St. Lawrence as far as the site of Montreal. Perhaps Cartier thought the broad St. Lawrence was the long-sought Northwest Passage, but years were to pass before men would fully understand the immense size of the new continent.

Cartier returned to the St. Lawrence for the third and last time to conquer an Indian tribe which he believed to possess great treasure. He did not succeed, and he did not find gold and other riches. He brought his ship back to France loaded with iron pyrites (called "fool's gold") and quartz crystals which he thought were diamonds. He did not find a Northwest Passage. But he did lay claim to vast new lands which were to be the foundation for "New France," an empire which explorers who followed him would carve out of the wilderness.

2. *The Fur Trade*

Then, for almost 60 years, France seemed to lose interest in the New World. There was, however, some trouble over the fishing waters in the North Atlantic off Newfoundland where Frenchmen had been fishing for more than 50 years. As fishermen from other countries began to enter the area, the French looked around for a place to dry their catch. They chose the Gaspe Peninsula, claimed for France by Cartier. While ashore, they began trading with the

Indians for furs and so began a colorful and important era in the history of America.

The fur trade was the foundation of New France and the North American beaver was the foundation of the fur trade. The beaver is an intelligent, hard-working animal which may grow to be more than two feet long and weigh more than 35 pounds. Most of its body is covered with fur so valuable that it has been hunted for hundreds of years. The fur is dark brown and has many long, stiff hairs which usually are plucked out. Underneath is another layer of short fur which is thick, soft and glossy.

Beaver pelts were in great demand in Europe because they were used to make hats called "beavers." French merchants began to realize the importance of a land which could supply these valuable pelts. In the early 1600s, the French decided to explore their new territories in earnest and set up fur-trading posts.

The men who came were not permanent settlers or empire-builders; they were explorers and adventurers. Their leaders were

Samuel de Champlain (1567-1635), a mapmaker turned explorer who came to the New World in 1603. Lake Champlain, which extends through the states of New York and Vermont into Canada, bears his name.

noblemen with colorful names and titles. With them came woodsmen, hunters, trappers, fur traders—restless common folk of many types. And always, almost from the very beginning, came the Church, the priests as adventurous as the rest but also determined to convert the Indians to the Catholic faith.

In 1603 France sent over an official, or viceroy, to govern the new territory. His name was Pierre du Gast, Sieur de Monts, and with him came Samuel de Champlain, a mapmaker who became a famous explorer. Within a few years Champlain had found the lake which bears his name in what is now New York State. He explored most of what is now New England; he sailed up the St. Lawrence River into Lake Ontario and Lake Huron. With him the exploring of the heart of the American continent began.

But Champlain was more than an explorer. He and De Monts were the first French colonizers in America. Champlain realized that the French would have to establish colonies if they wished to keep control of their New World possessions. The government in France did not agree with him.

France's chief interest in the New World during the 1600s was to use the land and its wealth, especially its luxurious fur pelts, for the benefit of France and her merchants there. So the government discouraged settlers from coming to the new land, preferring to leave the land and the fur trade entirely in the hands of strictly disciplined officials who would work with the Indians.

Nevertheless, Champlain helped to establish the first settlements in the northern part of North America. They were Quebec, in what is now Canada, and Port Royal, now called Annapolis Royal, in Nova Scotia.

Now maps began to go on sale in Paris showing the empire of New France in the wilderness of North America. So little was known about the territory that the maps were mere squiggles on parchment, but they showed New France stretching from Labra-

Jean Nicolet, dressed in Mandarin robes, steps ashore to greet people he believed were Chinese. Instead of China, however, he had landed in Green Bay, in what is now Wisconsin. The "Chinese" were friendly Winnebago Indians. The date is 1634.

dor south to the mouth of the Delaware River, and westward into the limitless reaches of the American continent.

3. *The Exploration of America's Heartland*

When Champlain became governor of New France in 1632, exploration of the territory was pushed forward. Jean Nicolet was among the first of these explorers who plunged excitedly into the vast wilderness of the country lying west and south of Quebec. They sought furs and they hoped to find other, untold riches. The country stretched on and on as they paddled west and south and it held who knew what great treasures? Most of all, they still hoped to find a Northwest Passage to China.

At one point, Nicolet thought he had found it. He was told by Indians around the Great Lakes that to the west there lived a race of people who were beardless and bald. Nicolet thought that surely these must be Chinese. Pointing his canoes westward, he pushed through the straits of Mackinac, skirted Lake Michigan's northern shore and entered Green Bay.

So certain was Nicolet that he was about to be ushered to the Chinese court that he and his men dressed in colorful Chinese robes of silk, embroidered with birds and flowers and topped by mandarin hats. Prudently, Nicolet also carried a pistol in each hand as he advanced to meet the "Chinese" but they turned out to be just another tribe of Indians. Instead of Cathay, Nicolet found only the rolling prairies of the Mississippi Valley and, perhaps, the Mississippi River itself.

Etienne Brule, who had come over as a boy with Champlain and has been called "the pioneer of pioneers," was the first European to see Lake Huron, the Sault Ste. Marie and Lake Superior.

Within a few years, two traders and a missionary became the first explorers to visit Minnesota. Pierre d'Esprit, Sieur de Radisson, and his brother-in-law, Medard Chouart, Sieur des Groseilliers, made a remarkable journey into the country south and west of Lake Superior. Many years later, Radisson wrote an amazing account of their explorations with vivid descriptions of the primitive life in the area. For instance, here is his description of a moose:

"He has a muzzle mighty bigge. I have scene some that have the nostrills so bigg that I putt into it my 2 fists att once with ease . . . He feeds like an ox . . . but seldom he galopps. I have scene some of their hornes that a man could not lift them from of the ground. They are branchy and flatt in the midle."

Radisson *(standing)* and Groseilliers *(seated)*, with their Indian guides, explored south and west of Lake Superior about 1660. This painting is by the famous American artist Frederic Remington.

Father Jacques Marquette, together with Louis Joliet, discovered the Mississippi River at Prairie du Chien, Wisconsin, June 17, 1673. This statue stands in Statuary Hall in the National Capitol at Washington, D.C. A granite monument at Ludington, Michigan, marks the site of Father Marquette's burial in May, 1675. Ottawa Indians reburied him in 1677 at a mission he founded at St. Ignace in Michigan's Upper Peninsula.

Marquette on the Mississippi, a U.S. postage stamp *(left)* issued on the occasion of the Trans-Mississippi Exposition of 1898. The Louisiana Purchase Commemorative stamp *(right)* was issued in 1904. The Louisiana territory, claimed by LaSalle for France, was sold to the United States in 1803 by Napoleon Bonaparte. This stamp shows the vast lands that became American by that purchase.

Other men followed quickly—traders, explorers, mapmakers, missionaries. Pere (Father) Jacques Marquette, a Jesuit missionary and skilled cartographer, and Louis Joliet, a trader and explorer, set out from the Straits of Mackinac in their long canoes, paddled down Lake Michigan, through Green Bay, and up the Fox River, then made the long portage in central Wisconsin to the Wisconsin River. They followed this river south to the Mississippi and thus pioneered a water route that later would lead hundreds of pioneers into the Mississippi Valley.

Marquette and Joliet followed the Mississippi as far south as the mouth of the Arkansas River, south of present-day Memphis, Tennessee. This was far enough to convince them that the river emptied into the Gulf of Mexico, rather than the Pacific Ocean, and was not the elusive Northwest Passage. So they turned their canoes about and headed back upstream. This time they turned off into the Illinois River, north of St. Louis, and eventually reached Lake Michigan. Thus, they pioneered another famed and still much-used water route. Joliet, Illinois, bears the name of the man who first explored its territory.

But it remained for one of the greatest explorers of them all to give form and substance to New France. He was Robert Cavelier,

Sieur de La Salle, an energetic, heroic man of vision and imagination—and also of great faults. La Salle, who has been called the "Prince of Explorers," was also bound, in the beginning, for China. He listened to the Indians' stories of a great river called the Ohio which flowed in the general direction of the Pacific and might be the long-sought passage to the Orient.

In a series of explorations, La Salle found the Ohio, traveled down it to the Mississippi and down the Mississippi to the Gulf of Mexico. Here, on the sands of the Gulf, he took possession of all the lands drained by the Mississippi in the name of the king of France. In honor of his king, Louis XIV, he named the territory Louisiana.

Robert Cavelier, Sieur de La Salle, stands at the Gulf of Mexico and claims all the lands drained by the Mississippi River for Louis XIV, King of France. He named the territory Louisiana.

Father Louis Hennepin discovers the Falls of St. Anthony, where Minneapolis, Minnesota, now stands. This painting by Douglas Volk hangs in the Minnesota State Capitol at St. Paul, Minnesota.

Father Louis Hennepin had come to the New World with La Salle and had been with him on several of his trips of exploration. While exploring Illinois, Hennepin was captured by the Indians and taken into the Minnesota country. There he discovered the Falls of St. Anthony, where Minneapolis is now. Hennepin seems to have specialized in waterfalls. He is also thought to be the first white man to see and to describe Niagara Falls.

La Salle must have eventually abandoned his vision of a passage to the Orient. He became convinced that some day this new land would be far wealthier than France. Like Champlain, however, he realized that France could not hold it simply by planting flags in virgin soil or burying in the ground leaden disks bearing the date and the arms of France. Settlers were needed to occupy such a vast area.

With the permission of the French government at Versailles, he established Fort Crevecoeur (Fort Heartbreak), near present-day Peoria. This was the first white settlement in what is now Illinois. He also established Fort Saint Louis, near Utica, Illinois. A small trading post on the southern tip of Lake Michigan eventually became Chicago. He built Fort Prud'homme where Memphis now stands.

Daniel Greysolon, Sieur du Luth, as depicted in a 9-foot bronze statue by the sculptor Jacques Lipchitz. The statue was unveiled on October 17, 1965. It stands on the Duluth campus of the University of Minnesota.

In 1684 La Salle went back to France for supplies and settlers for the colony he planned to establish at the mouth of the Mississippi. Returning with four ships and 200 colonists, La Salle made a fatal mistake. He landed at Matagorda Bay, in what is now Texas, thinking that this was the mouth of the Mississippi. He set out to march overland toward the Mississippi but on the way his followers mutinied and shot him.

La Salle was a man of vision and courage, but he also was proud, haughty, and inconsiderate of others. These faults finally brought to an end his own efforts to found a permanent and flourishing French colony in New France.

But other settlements — trading posts, for the most part — were springing up. La Salle himself had founded a settlement at Niagara. Fort Michilimackinac was established on Mackinac Island in the straits joining Lake Michigan and Lake Huron.

Daniel Greysolon, Sieur du Luth, visited the head of Lake Superior and the Minnesota country. He was another remarkable man. Bold and forceful, brave and capable, he has been called the "explorer-statesman" of the upper Mississippi Valley. He worked out treaties with the warring Indian tribes which made the area safe for the fur traders of France. The city of Duluth was named for him.

U.S. commemorative postage stamp issued in 1951 to mark the 250th anniversary of the landing of Antoine de la Mothe Cadillac at Detroit. The city's modern skyline appears in the background.

In the south, along the coast of the Gulf of Mexico, a number of forts and settlements were established by Pierre Le Moyne d'Iberville, a native of Montreal and one of 10 famous brothers.

In 1718, one brother, Jean Baptiste Le Moyne, Sieur de Bienville, founded the city which is regarded as the most "French" of all American cities — New Orleans.

There were other settlements — Detroit, founded by Antoine de la Mothe Cadillac, who left his name upon another city in Michigan, and, 200 years later, upon an automobile; St. Louis, Missouri; Fort Duquesne, where Pittsburgh is today. The French explored as far west as Montana and the Rocky Mountains and traded with the Indians of New Mexico.

Many of their forts were simply small stockades in the wilderness. One, Fort Beauharnois on the shores of Lake Pepin in Minnesota, was described by a Jesuit priest who saw it as "a plat of ground a hundred feet square surrounded by stakes twelve feet high with two good bastions." Three large log buildings stood within this enclosure, he reported.

The colorful and dramatic life of these explorers, trappers, and traders, and the missionaries who inevitably accompanied

Women did not often follow their husbands into the wilderness. Cadillac, however, wished to give his settlement at Detroit a sense of permanence. This painting by Robert A. Thom, shows Cadillac greeting his wife, Michigan's first pioneer woman.

them on their journeys, scarcely changed for more than 100 years. The white men, adventurous, daring, gay and imaginative, "weare Caesars," as Radisson wrote, in the land of the primitive Indians.

The French were quick to learn from the Indians, to use their canoes, to dip their paddles into the lakes and rivers and streams long used by the red men to criss-cross the huge territory of New France. They lived with the Indians, married Indian women, learned from the Indians the ways of the beaver and muskrat. If they exploited the Indians — and they did — as a means of gathering the great bales of furs which eventually found their way to France, the French also treated the Indians better than did most white men from other nations.

With the French flair for being practical, the fur trade was

Canoe Shooting the Rapids by Frances Ann Hopkins, the wife of a fur trader. This was the typical canoe used for over 100 years on the Great Lakes. Sixteen canoemen were needed to control the boat, and there was still additional space for passengers and cargo.

strictly organized and closely supervised. Control was in the hands of several companies to which the king of France had given royal monopolies. Since these companies were not interested in populating New France, settlers were discouraged from coming to America, in spite of the wisdom of such men as ·La Salle and Champlain.

Nevertheless, independent colonists did slip across the Atlantic, and many worked on their own as fur traders, becoming coureurs de bois ("racers" or "runners of the woods"). This means that they originally operated illegally, and the authorities did their best to stop such trading. But it went on for the coureurs de bois knew the deep forests. In time they became as much a part of the legend of the fur trade as the voyageurs ("travelers"). These latter were sturdy woodsmen and boatmen who paddled the great canoes and carried the heavy packs on portage, transporting men and goods for the fur trade.

Under such great leaders as Louis de Buade, Comte de Frontenac, who was governor of New France during the latter part of the 17th century, the French achieved a firm grip upon all the vital waterways west of the Appalachian Mountains. The only great river not under French control was the Hudson.

The entire "west" of that era was French but, with their far-flung network of trading posts and settlements, the French had spread themselves too thin. The question now was whether or not they could hold what they had won during the long years of daring exploration and high adventure.

4. *The Loss of New France*

The creation of New France had not been entirely peaceful. From the very beginning, the French fought with other rival powers of Europe, chiefly the English, to keep their bases in the New World and their control of the fur trade. In these continuing wars, the Indians played an important part. Some of the powerful tribes fought on the side of the English; others for the French. The struggle was bitter and long, lasting more than 100 years. Each flareup of fighting reflected a new outbreak in the long war in Europe between England and France.

The final struggle in America began in 1754 with the French and Indian War. The settlers in the East, along the Atlantic coast, were English or living in colonies ruled by the British government. These colonists began to push ever westward toward the fertile lands of the Ohio Valley. Great Britain also had long claimed these lands of New France. Eventually the rival claims could only be settled by force of arms.

The French, who had lived and worked and inter-married with the Indians for so many generations, had done their work well

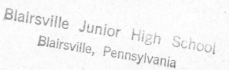

in cementing alliances with the powerful and warlike tribes. Most of the Indians, seeing that the French meant to keep the forests and prairies in their natural state, while the English colonists would clear them and plow the ground to plant crops, fought on the side of the French.

But the British also had allies among the Indians, and the fighting was bitter and bloody, with all the brutality and savagery of Indian warfare. In 1759, the British army under General James Wolfe advanced upon the city of Quebec defended by 15,000 French troops under Louis Joseph, Marquis de Montcalm. After a three-month siege, the British troops, under cover of a cloudy night, scaled the steep cliffs to the Plains of Abraham, a plateau fortified by the French. There, in a short battle, the French were defeated. Both Wolfe and Montcalm were killed.

When the war ended, France had lost her empire in the New World. The Treaty of Paris, signed in 1763, gave to Great Britain what is now Canada and all the land east of the Mississippi with the exception of New Orleans. France then ceded New Orleans to Spain, along with all the land west of the Mississippi. Of its great colonial empire, France kept only two small islands near Newfoundland for use as fishing stations.

Today, New France is simply a name on old maps and in history books. Of the French who lived there, some went to Quebec which to this day has remained strongly French in language, customs and spirit. Some stayed behind, mingling with the new settlers as they had earlier with the Indians, intermarrying and blending into the population until their French identity often was lost.

But they left behind them a rich tradition of brave men who sang in the wilderness, who wore jaunty caps often trimmed with fur and tied bright sashes around their waists, who wore the moccasins of the Indian, who loved to float in their canoes upon the clear lakes and streams or wander in the solitude of the forests, who sat

The 200th anniversary of the British victory at Fort Duquesne during the French and Indian War is commemorated in this U.S. stamp issued in 1958. The troops which captured the fort in 1758 included a young Virginia colonel named George Washington. He is shown on horseback in the center.

around their camp fires at night, smoking their pipes and exchanging stories.

They left behind fragments of their language — their own names or those of their rulers, their patron saints, their leaders — on such places as St. Paul, New Orleans, St. Louis, Vincennes.

They also left behind names which expressed their love of the wilderness — Lac Qui Parle ("lake that talks"); Eau Claire ("clear water"); Flambeau (river and lake, recalling fishing there by "flambeau" or torchlight); Belpre ("beautiful prairie"); Bois Brule ("burned timber"); Boise ("wooded"); Bonpas (a prairie "good to walk on").

Other men and women would follow the French trail-blazers into the Ohio Valley and the Mississippi Valley. The forests would be cleared and planted to crops. The ashes of the old camp fires would be scattered or turned under by the plows cutting into the soil. But the heritage from the French would remain. And in the meantime, thousands of other French men and women, refugees from religious persecution in Europe, were finding a place for themselves in the New World.

PART II.

The Huguenots

1. *Religious Conflict in France*

Not many years after Jacques Cartier discovered the St. Lawrence, changes were taking place in France that would greatly influence the history of the French in America.

These changes were brought about by the Reformation, the movement sweeping Europe which sought to reform the Roman Catholic church. This struggle was not entirely religious; the Reformation had many other causes which had to do with the complicated politics of Europe. Catholic France was caught up in it as more and more of her people began to accept the teachings of John Calvin, a Frenchman who fled to Switzerland and became one of the great Protestant leaders of the 1500s.

The French Protestants were called Huguenots and, since they grew strong in number and influence, they were the center of political and religious quarrels in France for more than 30 years. In 1562, a group of Huguenots tried to settle in South Carolina but abandoned their colony two years later.

In 1564, another group tried again. They established Fort Caroline near the mouth of the St. John's River, not far from the site of present-day Jacksonville, Florida. This was in territory claimed by Spain and the Spaniards, who were loyal Catholics, were not long in resenting the intrusion—and by Protestants, too. A party of Spaniards landed and slaughtered all but a few of the Huguenots "as heretic interlopers and not as Frenchmen," as the Spanish commander said.

Two years later, a French Catholic nobleman revenged the French. He invaded Florida and hanged "not as Spaniards but as murderers" all the Spaniards he and his men could find. So ended, for a time, Huguenot settlements in America.

But in France, persecutions continued. One of the most tragic events of all the religious conflicts which ripped Europe from one end to the other was the Massacre of St. Bartholomew's Day— August 24, 1572. Catherine de'Medici, mother of the boy king of France, feared the growing power of the Huguenots, who now included some of the greatest names in France, such as the Admiral Gaspard de Coligny. On that day in August, when prominent men and women from all over France were in Paris for the marriage of Henry of Navarre, a Huguenot leader, to the sister of the French king, the gates of the city were barred and soldiers fell upon the Huguenots, killing many of them, including Admiral Coligny and other important leaders.

From this time on, Huguenots began leaving France. In 1594, Henry of Navarre became king. Because France was a Catholic country, he considered it wise to become a Catholic himself. But he did not forget the Huguenots and four years later he issued the Edict of Nantes, one of history's most famous royal decrees. The Huguenots were granted freedom to worship as they pleased and regained their civil liberties. This put an end, for the time being, to the religious wars. The Huguenots were allowed to fortify certain cities which were their chief centers. La Rochelle, a seaport in the west of France on the Bay of Biscay, was one of the most famous of the Huguenot cities.

2. *The French Protestant Emigration*

The Huguenots were a remarkable group of people. For the most part they were merchants, businessmen, skilled workers and artisans. They were men of ability and, often, of wealth. Many were members of the aristocracy. They formed what almost seemed to be a Protestant republic within a Catholic country.

To a later king, Louis XIV, they seemed to be a threat and he decided to wipe them out. He began by taking away the privileges granted them by the Edict of Nantes. With this action in 1685, called the Revocation of the Edict of Nantes, persecution began again and with it came the "Great Dispersion" — the flight of thousands of Huguenots from France.

Not many of them came to America at first, however. The French kings, with their eyes on their empire of "New France" in the American wilderness — an empire which was predominently Catholic — were not willing to see strong French Protestant colonies spring up in the New World. For a time the Huguenots were not allowed to emigrate to America, although groups of them still managed to slip out of the French ports. More of them, however, fled to neighboring Protestant countries, such as England, Holland, Switzerland and parts of Germany. There they met other groups, some of them religious dissenters like themselves, others simply adventurous men and women seeking fresh opportunity in a New World. The Huguenots often cast their lot with these groups.

It is not easy to trace the Huguenot migrations to America, either because they came with other groups or because their names frequently changed. They often were misspelled, carelessly written, badly pronounced or simply translated into another language. For instance, a Frenchman named Le Blanc fled into Holland, where he became known as DeWitt. If he had gone to England, he might have been called White. Letellier became Tailor in England, Le Roy became King and Le Brun was called Brown.

The Huguenot-Walloon Tercentenary (300th anniversary) half dollar commemorates the arrival of the French Protestants and the French-speaking Protestants of Belgium in New Amsterdam. One side of the coin carries the profiles of Admiral Gaspard de Coligny, one of the French Huguenots' great leaders and martyrs, and William the Silent, king of Holland. William was an early leader of the Protestant Reformation in Europe and his fourth wife was Admiral de Coligny's daughter. The other side of the coin shows the *New Netherland*, the ship which brought the colonists to the New World.

Probably no more than 15,000 Huguenots came to what is now the United States, most of them between 1685 and about 1760. Yet, these Huguenots formed one of the few major "waves" of French immigration in the 400-year history of the French in America. The French never have been great "migrators," even to their own colonies. They did come in small groups for special reasons — to explore or to trade in furs, for instance — as did the men of New France.

The Huguenot-Walloon Tercentenary stamp issue of 1924. These, also, were issued to commemorate the 300th anniversary of the landing of these French and Belgium Protestants. The 1-cent stamp shows their ship, the *New Netherland*. The 2-cent stamp depicts their landing at Albany, New York. The 5-cent stamp portrays the Ribault Memorial Monument at Mayport, Florida, where the Huguenots had tried to establish a colony 60 years earlier.

They came as refugees from later political upheavals in France or to pursue special careers in America. But the fact was that, for the most part, life in France was not only pleasant but stimulating. For long periods the intellectual climate permitted freedom of ideas, so that French men and women were not especially eager to leave their native land.

The Huguenots, of course, were forced out by religious intolerance and persecution. They brought to the New World their skills, their ability as businessmen, their belongings and their money, or as much of it as they could take with them. In short, they came to stay. And, while it is difficult to trace them because they often came from Holland bearing Dutch names, from England with English names or from Germany with German names, nevertheless their contribution to the founding of our country was so outstanding that it has been well recorded. The Huguenots furnished America with some of its ablest citizens. Perhaps no other group of non-English-speaking people has contributed more to American life.

But in the beginning, the French were not always welcome everywhere. For many colonists, the picture was darkened by bitterness toward the Frenchmen of New France, their alliance with the Indians and the horrors of Indian warfare. The settlers did not forget, for instance, that the Deerfield Massacre in Massachusetts was directed by one Hertel de Rouville. Perhaps they did forget that the colonists, led by the English and using their own Indian allies, often struck back in kind.

But the Huguenots, after all, were Protestants and kindred sufferers under religious oppression. Eventually they were accepted as "honest, reliable folk." Wherever they settled, they brought a gaiety and buoyancy to life which was very much a part of their French heritage. This was especially noticeable in the stern, austere atmosphere of Puritan New England. The Puritans mistrusted beauty but the French showed their love for it in such things as the cultivation of flowers. The Puritans did not celebrate Christmas and the French did, with all the joyousness of the Gallic tradition.

In spite of their differences, the Huguenots and the Puritans apparently got along very well indeed. This was generally true in the other colonies where the Huguenots settled, and, by the time the second generation had grown to manhood, they were thoroughly caught up in the life of the American colonies. They displayed the gift of the French for intermarrying and blending with the people of the new land. Some of the most famous names in American history belong to men and women of Huguenot ancestry.

Almost all of the 13 colonies received at least a few Huguenot families at some time during the years before the American Revolution. Their major settlements, however, were in Massachusetts, Maine, New Jersey, New York, Pennsylvania, Delaware, Virginia and South Carolina.

The Mayflower, with its band of English Pilgrims, had carried some Huguenots who had settled in Leyden, Holland, and met the Pilgrims during their exile there. One was a young French girl named Priscilla Mullins, the heroine of the famous love affair involving John Alden and Miles Standish. Priscilla's last name originally was Molines. She sailed on the Mayflower with her father, mother and brother, all of whom died during the first winter in New England. Other Huguenot passengers on the Mayflower included the Mullins' servant, Robert Carter (perhaps his name originally was Cartier) and Samuel Terry.

Two years after the Revocation of the Edict of Nantes, about 150 Huguenot families came to Massachusetts. Several other groups settled in Rhode Island and Maine. A French Protestant church was organized in Boston to which the general court of the colony voted 12 pounds from the public treasury "for their encouragement as strangers and for carrying on the public worship of God amongst them."

The Huguenot Monument,
Oxford, Massachusetts.

The inscription reads:
In Memory of
the
Huguenots
Exiles for Their Faith
Who Made The First Settlement
of
Oxford
1687
"We Live Not for Ourselves Only
But For Posterity"

One well-known Huguenot settlement in Massachusetts was at
Oxford or New Oxford, near what is now Worcester. In 1687, about
30 families settled on a grant of 2,500 acres but the history of the
settlement was not a happy one. In those days, it was located on the

frontier and prey to Indian attacks. Some of the people were massacred; others left in discouragement and returned to Boston. Today, all that remains is a monument.

In 1686, some 50 families settled Frenchtown in what is now Rhode Island but their fate was unhappy, too. Their title to their land was challenged. Next, war broke out between the English and the French of New France and the Huguenots fell under suspicion, mainly because they were French. The settlement was attacked and virtually destroyed by a mob from nearby Greenwich. Some of the families moved to Boston; others to New York.

A colorful Huguenot settled at Salem, Massachusetts. He was Philippe L'Anglois, whose name was speedily changed to its English version — Philip English. He became wealthy and was one of the earliest of Salem's important merchants. He built a mansion known as "English's great house." Somehow, during the Salem witchcraft madness, both English and his wife were accused of witchcraft and thrown into prison. Friends managed to have them transferred to a prison in Boston and there they escaped, probably with official help. When the witchcraft hysteria had died down, English returned to Salem and lived out his life there.

3. *Huguenots in Colonial America*

From these and other Huguenots came some of the distinguished men and women of New England. Many had settled originally at Oxford before being forced to scatter to other parts of New England. There was Gabriel Bernon who owned much of the land at Oxford and was the settlement's chief businessman, although he himself lived in Boston. Bernon, who later became a prominent citizen of Rhode Island, started a "chamoiserie" at Oxford, a "wash-leather" factory which dressed animal skins for shipping to the glove-makers of France.

There were Jean, Benjamin and Andre Faneuil who came from

Faneuil Hall, Boston, called the "cradle of liberty" because it was a meeting place of patriots during the American Revolution. It was built in 1742.

La Rochelle to settle in Boston. They were successful merchants and, eventually, ardent colonial patriots. Andre died in 1728 and 1,100 people attended his funeral. Guns on the ships in Boston harbor fired a last salute.

Peter (Pierre) Faneuil, Andre's nephew and heir to his sizeable fortune, was, next to John Hancock, the leading merchant of Massachusetts. It was he who gave Boston the public market house called Faneuil Hall, the "cradle of liberty." It stands there today, in a section of the city which long since has become a haven for other, newer immigrants to America. Peter Faneuil, who died in 1743, became Boston's richest merchant. John Lowell preached his funeral oration.

James Bowdoin, whose name had acquired an English spelling, was the son of Pierre Baudouin, another immigrant from La Rochelle. James also became one of Boston's leading merchants and was a member of the Colonial Council for several years. When he died, he left one of the largest estates of any one person in the colony. His son, another James, was a distinguished statesman and patriot, a fellow agitator, with Samuel Adams and John Hancock, for independence for the American colonies.

During the Revolution, the second James Bowdoin served as president of the Massachusetts Constitutional Convention. Later he became governor of Massachusetts. Bowdoin College in Maine, where the family had large holdings, was named for him. He was the first president of the American Academy of Arts and Sciences. His son, still another James, served as minister to Spain in 1804.

Another prominent Huguenot, R. H. Dana, was a writer, editor and founder of the *North American Review*. His son, R. H. Dana, Jr., was the author of the classic, *Two Years before the Mast*. This

These portraits portray three generations of the eminent Bowdoin family of Boston, father, son, and grandson. James Bowdoin I *(left)*, was a wealthy merchant and Colonial leader. He was the son of Pierre Baudouin, an immigrant from La Rochelle, France. The family's last name acquired an English spelling. The portrait was painted in 1747 by Joseph Badger. James Bowdoin II *(center)*, was a distinguished statesman of the American Revolutionary War period. He was later governor of Massachusetts. Bowdoin College in Maine is named for him. James Bowdoin III *(right)*, was minister to Spain in 1804. This portrait is by Gilbert Stuart, the most famous early American artist.

Paul Revere was 78 years old when Gilbert Stuart painted this portrait of him in 1813. The stamp was issed in 1958.

family also produced Charles A. Dana, one of America's great newspapermen and editor of the *New York Sun.*

The historian who wrote that the Huguenots were "a hotbed of talent" does not seem to have been wrong.

One of the most famous of American patriots, Paul Revere, was a Huguenot. He was born in Boston. His father's name was Apollos Rivoire. Paul Revere has been best remembered for his famous "midnight ride," which he made as official messenger, or courier, of the Massachusetts Provincial Assembly which had decided to watch every move made by the British and their troops. Earlier, Revere had taken part in the Boston Tea Party and later he served as an officer in the Massachusetts militia.

Like his father before him, Revere was a silversmith. He designed and printed the first Continental money issued by the Congress which was organized to conduct the Revolutionary War. He was a fine artist and craftsman and today the silver and copper pieces which he made are highly prized and are exhibited in art museums throughout the United States.

A mural in Boston depicts how Paul Revere might have delivered his warning to the citizens of Lexington. At the time of this event Revere was 40 years old and had already taken part in the Boston Tea Party.

Another famous New Englander should be mentioned here because, although he lived during the 19th century, he was of Huguenot descent. He was John Greenleaf Whittier. His mother's family name had originally been "Feuillevert," the French word for "green leaf."

New York was another center of Huguenot settlement. Small groups of French Protestants had been coming to what is now New York State since 1623 when it was founded by the Dutch as New Netherland. Peter Minuit, first governor of the colony, is thought to have been a Huguenot. The formidable Peter Stuyvesant, peg-legged governor of the colony, married a Huguenot, Judith Bayard. The first doctor in New Amsterdam (New York City) was French and so was the first school teacher. The first white child born there — Jean Vigne — was a Huguenot.

The French Protestants in the Netherlands were called Walloons, rather than Huguenots. They had come from the area of northern France which is now Belgium and had fled from there into Holland to escape persecution. And so it is that many men and women now living in New York who regard themselves as descendants of the early Dutch settlers, actually have French blood as well. The French and the Dutch seem to have mingled happily — demonstrating once again, perhaps, the French talent for assimilating. The great Knickerbocker families, who settled in Dutchess county north of New York City and were the subject of Washington Irving's many tales, represent a blend of French and Dutch blood.

Within 30 years after the arrival of the first settlers, all proclamations in New Amsterdam were issued in French as well as Dutch. The new settlers were happy. They founded a church, "L'Eglise du St. Esprit" (the Church of the Holy Spirit) which stands today and is known in New York City as "the French Church."

Their glowing letters, carried back to Holland, brought more settlers, both Dutch and French. One such letter describes the new land to which they had come:

The 250th anniversary of the founding of New Rochelle, New York, is commemorated by this half dollar issued in 1938. One side of the coin shows John Pell, "Lord of Pelham Manor," who sold 6,000 acres of land to the Huguenots. The "fatted calf" recalls a portion of the sale agreement whereby Pell and his heirs should receive on demand "one fatte calf on every fouer and twentyth day of June Yearly and Every Years forever." The other side of the coin depicts a fleur-de-lis, the symbol of France. This flower appears on the shield of the French city of La Rochelle, from which the settlers came, and also on the shield of the city of New Rochelle, New York.

"We were much gratified on arriving in this country. Here we found beautiful rivers, bubbling fountains flowing down into the valleys, basins of running waters in the flatlands, agreeable fruits in the woods, such as strawberries, walnuts, and wild grapes. The woods abound with venison. There is considerable fish in the rivers, good tillage land; here is, especially, free coming and going, without fear of the naked natives of the country. Had we cows, hogs, and other cattle fit for food—which we expect in the first ships—we would not wish to return to Holland."

One of the early settlers was Isaac Bethlo, or Bedloe, who was born in Calais in northern France, and arrived in New Netherland in 1652. Bedloe's Island in New York harbor was named for him. Almost 250 years later, this island became the site of the Statue of Liberty, the gift of France to the United States.

Perhaps the most remarkable Huguenot settlement in the northern colonies was at New Rochelle, New York. The town was founded in 1688 under the leadership of David Bonrepos, the minister, and it soon became the most important center of French culture in the New England area. The families who settled there —more than 20 French families by 1695—determined to keep alive "the manners of the mother country" and something of the charm and refinement of life in France.

For parents who wished their sons to learn the French language and the gentle manners of polite French society, New Rochelle was the place to send them. Its schools, both boarding schools and day schools, had excellent reputations. Dancing was taught. During the week, tableaux and short comedies were given. Young ladies were taught the "ladylike accomplishments" of singing and music, embroidery and painting and etiquette.

Such famous Americans as John Jay, Philip Schuyler, Washington Irving and Gouverneur Morris were sent to New Rochelle when they were schoolboys. During these years, the French women of New Rochelle also made an enduring contribution to American life with their invention of the rag carpet.

Eventually, New Rochelle became quite thoroughly Americanized. But the Huguenots in another settlement in New Netherland clung to their French heritage longer and more stubbornly. New Pfaltz, or Nouveau Palatinat, had been named in honor of the help given Huguenot refugees in the area of Mannheim, in the Palatinate section of Germany. New Pfaltz, a village with a German name, remained French until after the American Revolution, longer than any other French settlement in what is now New York.

Huguenots began to come to Pennsylvania and Delaware during the 1650s and 1660s. There was steady emigration to this area, especially after 1681 when what is now Pennsylvania was granted to William Penn. The history of these immigrants is hard to trace because most of the French Huguenots who came to Pennsylvania had lived for a time in Alsace-Lorraine and the German provinces and, once again, they did not always keep their French names.

Delliker once was de la Cour and the Kieffers were descended from the Tonnelliers. The unique ability of the French to adapt themselves to new homes and new conditions of living works against them, making it extremely difficult at times to trace their considerable contribution to the settlement of what is now the United States.

A Huguenot heroine, Marie Ferree, became Marie Fuhre in Germany. When her husband died, this remarkable woman took her family to England and sought out William Penn, who was impressed and agreed to let her have a tract of 2,000 acres in Pennsylvania. He even took her to see Queen Anne, who promised "substantial aid" and kept her promise. The name of Marie Ferree's son seems to be recorded as Fiere, although most of her other descendants managed to keep the correct French spelling.

Historians who have carefully studied the Huguenot emigra-

Gouverneur Morris (1752-1816). He was born and died at Morrisana, New York. His services to the American Revolution were distinguished. He was a member of Congress from New York, 1776; one of the committee drafting the Constitution, 1787; U.S. Minister to France, 1792-1794; U.S. Senator from New York, 1800-1803.

tion have decided that more French settlers, especially Huguenots, came to Pennsylvania than to any other colony, with the possible exception of South Carolina. This was partly due to the enterprising William Penn, as well as later developers of the colony, all of whom sent out quite a bit of advertising material in French to encourage settlers to come to the colony. A special act giving relief to Huguenots in distress or difficulty was passed in Pennsylvania as late as 1797, long after most of the Huguenot immigration had ended.

Two interesting Frenchmen who came to America during these years just before the Revolution and who are associated with the Pennsylvania area are Michel Guillaume Jean de Crevecoeur and Anthony Benezet.

Crevecoeur was born in Normandy in northern France and educated partially, at least, in England. He came to New France in the 1750s and journeyed around the Ohio River and Great Lakes area. Ten years later, he traveled through New York, New Jersey and Pennsylvania. Eventually he married and settled down on a farm in what is now Orange County, New Jersey. There he did the work which made him famous — a series of essays published as a book in London in 1782. These *Letters from an American Farmer* form one of the most complete records of life in America during the colonial years before the Revolution.

Benezet also was born in northern France and educated partially in London. An idealist who tried hard to right some of the many social wrongs of the 18th century, Benezet was filled with pity and indignation over the plight of the Negro slaves in America. He wanted the slaves freed and was one of America's earliest abolitionists. He began a long and continuous correspondence with the distinguished men and women of his era — Benjamin Franklin, the queens of France, Portugal and England, even Frederick the Great of Prussia. He opened a night school for Negroes and taught in it himself. In 1766, he published a small book, *A Caution and Warning to Great Britain and Her Colonies on the Calamitous State of the Enslaved Negroes*—a book which aroused much interest in the American colonies, and was the first antislavery book published in America. Late in life, he became greatly concerned with the plight of the American Indians.

Between 1619 and 1621 a tiny group of Huguenots had been brought to Virginia to plant vineyards and cultivate the wild grapes growing in the area. Colonists and merchant promoters clung to the idea that the vine could be grown anywhere along the eastern coast of America. This settlement apparently simply disappeared. But other settlers came, most of them sent by the Virginia Company of London, a group of "noblemen, gentlemen, and merchants." The company was granted a charter by King James I of England for the settlement of south Virginia. The investors, and the French Huguenots themselves, expected to transplant the great industries of France, such as wine-making and the weaving of silk, to the New World. Consequently, the governor of Virginia also was told "to plant Mulberry trees and make silk, and take care of the Frenchmen sent about that work." This experiment did not succeed in Virginia. Like the other settlers, the French quickly began to grow tobacco instead.

The Huguenots did develop a reputation for making excellent wine in the area around their best-known settlement in Virginia— Manakintown, 20 miles northwest of present-day Richmond, on the James River. These colonists had been sent out from England by King William III in 1690, after the Revocation of the Edict of Nantes. The British were actively helping the French Huguenot refugees to emigrate to America. In Virginia, the Huguenots were given free land and exempted from paying taxes for seven years. Many members of the House of Burgesses, the ruling body of Virginia, contributed privately to help the refugees.

4. *The Huguenots of South Carolina*

But it was in South Carolina that the largest group of French immigrants settled. And they were an extraordinary group — intelligent, cultured, enterprising and prosperous. At first the other settlers, mostly of English origin, resented them. For awhile, the French were not allowed to take part in the government of the colony, but after some years they were accepted. Perhaps no other group of "Americans" contributed more heroes and statesmen to the colonial era and the Revolutionary War than did these French Huguenots from the Carolinas.

King Charles II of England encouraged a group of Huguenot exiles living in England to come to South Carolina in 1679 to raise grapes, olives and silkworms. Others came during the next six years but the great flood of Huguenot immigration into South Carolina came after the Revocation in 1685.

Charleston became the largest and richest Huguenot settlement in South Carolina. The French also settled along the Santee River north of Charleston and in such numbers that the river for many years was called the "French Santee." Here there were "vast Ciprus-Trees, of which the French make Canoes, that will carry fifty or sixty barrels." These "canoes," with their two masts and Bermuda sails, were used to travel up and down the Atlantic coast between the Santee and Charleston. Along the Santee, the French established plantations where they produced rice, cotton and indigo. Their houses were spacious and of brick and stone.

An early historian, writing in 1700, describes the French who were living along the Santee and hints that jealousy was perhaps one reason for resentment toward them on the part of the English:

"(He found) seventy Families living on this (Santee) River, who live as Decently and Happily, as any Planters in these Southward parts of America. The French, being a temperate Industrious People some of them bringing very little of Effects, yet by their endeavors and Mutual Assistance amongst themselves (which is highly to be Commended) have outstrip't our English, who brought with them Larger Fortunes, tho' as it seems less endeavor to manage their Talent to the best Advantage."

In Charleston, entire streets were occupied by Huguenots who built up towering fortunes. Their early poverty was simply typical of exiles moving from the Old World to the New and unable to take much with them. But the Huguenots in South Carolina, and elsewhere in the American colonies never were destitute immigrants. And they were thrifty and progressive. By the time of the American Revolution, one member of a famous South Carolina Huguenot family, Gabriel Manigault, was able to loan 220,000 pounds sterling to the colonial government for carrying on the war. He ranks with Gouverneur Morris, another Huguenot, as a financier of the Revolution.

The Huguenots of Charleston lived in lovely homes and preserved much of the cultural and intellectual life for which France was famous. The city had private schools and French-language newspapers. But that outstanding characteristic of the French, the ability to assimilate, could already be seen. Although French Huguenots were coming into South Carolina as late as the 1760's, the older families had become as Anglo-Saxon as the English. They quickly merged into the lawyer-planter social class of the colony and only their French accents set them apart for a time.

5. *Huguenot Patriots and Political Leaders*

Francis Marion was a South Carolinian who was a hero of the Revolutionary War. He was the cavalry leader whom the British called "the old swamp fox." General Marion took part in one of the first battles of the war. Later he organized a force of raiders known as "Marion's Brigade." They could come and go as he needed them and always were ready to take up their arms and leap on their horses on short notice. Some were the best shots and the best riders in the colony. They attacked often and disrupted British communications

General Francis Marion *(at right)* with some of his men.

Marion's Brigade crossing the Pedee River in South Carolina (1778) to attack the British forces under Banastre Tarleton.

so completely that it was impossible for troops in the Carolinas to keep in touch with each other. Although the British hunted him without ceasing, Marion never was caught. After the war, he served in the South Carolina state senate and lived out his life quietly on his plantation.

Most of the Huguenots were ardent patriots and supporters of independence from Great Britain. Some, however, did remain loyal to the British crown. After all, great numbers had fled to England as refugees from France, had been treated well by the British government and even helped considerably to make a start in the New World. In the early years in America, it was vital to the Huguenots' survival that they submerge themselves in the life of the British colonies. For some, their sympathies were with Britain as a country which had spent so many years fighting France, the country which had persecuted them.

As the Huguenots merged into the English population of the colonies, their faith began to change, too. At first, following the classic tradition of religious refugees, they established their churches as one of their acts in the New World. These churches were of the Reformed or Calvinist faith but very soon they were absorbed into the Church of England. The French talent for assimilation extended even to matters of faith and the Church of England was the Established Church — although in New England the buoyant French were somewhat out of sympathy with the Puritans' dour point of view concerning things of the soul. There was another reason for the changeover. In the 17th and 18th centuries, the Church of England was greatly influenced by the teachings of John Calvin.

During the years of the American Revolution and the welding of the 13 colonies into a sovereign nation, many more French Huguenots played important roles. There was the Reverend Jacob Duche who opened the first Continental Congress with prayer. There were John Jay, Henry Laurens and Elias Boudinot, all of whom served as presidents of the Continental Congress. John Laurens, Henry's son, was an aide-de-camp of George Washington.

John Jay, who eventually became the first Chief Justice of the United States Supreme Court, had a long and distinguished career as lawyer and statesman. He worked with John Adams and Benjamin Franklin in drawing up the Treaty of Paris which ended the Revolutionary War, and, with Henry Laurens, was one of the signers of the treaty. He was minister to Spain during the Revolution and later served as secretary of foreign affairs until President Washington named him Chief Justice.

In 1794, Washington appointed him special ambassador to Great

Henry Laurens, one of the Colonial leaders of Huguenot ancestry who served as president of the Continental Congress. He was also a signer of the Treaty of Paris which ended the Revolutionary War.

John Jay, painted by Gilbert Stuart. He was another French Huguenot who served as president of the Continental Congress. He later became the first Chief Justice of the United States, helped draw up the Treaty of Paris, negotiated the Jay Treaty with England, and was governor of New York.

Britain and assigned him the task of negotiating a new treaty with the British, known as the Jay Treaty, which was designed to settle disputes which had arisen between the two countries as the result of the war.

A year later, Jay resigned as Chief Justice to become governor of New York. He was one of the few men in United States history

Alexander Hamilton, born in the West Indies but reared in America, was of Huguenot ancestry through his mother's family. He became the new nation's first Secretary of the Treasury and established a national bank and a mint for coining money.

to resign from the Supreme Court for another post in government. He retired in 1801.

Alexander Hamilton, who became the first Secretary of the Treasury of the United States, was of Huguenot descent through his mother's family. He had been born in the West Indies but educated in America. During the war, he fought bravely in the New Jersey campaign, then became Washington's secretary with the rank of lieutenant colonel.

After the war, Hamilton studied law, represented New York in the Congress of the Confederation and played an active part in the Constitutional Convention of 1787 which framed the constitution of the United States. As Secretary of the Treasury, Hamilton established a national bank and a mint for coining money. His management of the new nation's financial problems started the country on the way to prosperity.

When Washington retired as President, Hamilton helped him prepare his Farewell Address. Hamilton's own life ended tragically. In 1804, he became involved in a dispute with his bitter political rival, Aaron Burr, who was Vice President of the United States under Thomas Jefferson. Burr challenged Hamilton to a duel and Hamilton was killed.

Elias Boudinot, as president of the Continental Congress, signed the Treaty of Paris after it had been ratified by the Congress. In 1795, he became director of the mint established by Hamilton. Another Huguenot, Michael Hilligas, became first treasurer of the United States.

Such was just a small part of the contribution made by the French Huguenots to the founding of the United States. The Revolution also brought a new group of Frenchmen to America. They came in the form of the army and navy of a foreign nation, France itself, but some stayed. And they were followed, once again, by others, many of them victims of political persecutions.

PART III.

Revolutions and Refugees

1. *France Aids the American Revolutionaries*

France often has been called America's "oldest ally" because she came to the help of the struggling colonists during their fight for independence from Great Britain. At the beginning of the American Revolution in 1775, France held back, although American leaders soon sought her help. Louis XVI of France and his advisors would have been delighted to see the English lose their American colonies, just as France had lost her territory to England some 10 years earlier, but they did not wish to become involved in a losing war.

However, during the first three years of the war, a steady stream of supplies and ammunition found its way from French ports to the colonies. In 1777, the most famous Frenchman in American history, Marie Joseph Paul Roch Yves Gilbert du Motier, Marquis de Lafayette, also crossed the Atlantic. Filled with enthusiasm for the colonists' fight for liberty — and also by his own youthful desire for glory — he had abandoned family, wife and the career of a member of the French nobility to come to America.

The Continental Congress in Philadelphia did not receive him with open arms. Members were suspicious, remembering earlier

The most famous Frenchman in American history was the Marquis de Lafayette. He was not quite 20 years of age when he crossed the Atlantic to join the American colonists' fight for independence.

A U.S. commemorative stamp *(left)* was issued in 1952 to mark the 175th anniversary of Lafayette's arrival in America. The French flag appears on the right. Another American commemorative stamp *(right)* was issued in 1957 to mark the 200th anniversary of Lafayette's birth on September 6, 1757. The likeness is from a portrait by Court, now hanging in the museum at Versailles, France. On the left is a Revolutionary War rifle, and on the right the sword presented to Lafayette by the U.S. Government.

"volunteers," many of them French and most of them adventurers and soldiers of fortune seeking military rank and profit.

But Congress was stunned by the tall, red-haired Marquis' request. Although he did want the rank of a major general, he did not want a command. He asked only to be "near the person of General Washington till such time as he may think proper to entrust me with a division of the army."

"After the sacrifices I have made, I have the right to expect two favours; one is to serve at my own expense — the other is to serve, at first, as volunteer" — so said Lafayette.

Washington and the young Frenchman, who was not yet 20, formed a deep and enduring friendship. Lafayette served at the

The Washington-Lafayette silver dollar, struck on December 14, 1899, the 100th anniversary of Washington's death. The statue of Lafayette on horseback that is depicted was erected in Paris with money contributed by school children of the United States.

Battle of Brandywine, where he was wounded. He lived through the dreadful winter at Valley Forge with the colonial troops. Finally, it was under Lafayette's command that a small group of American troops operating in Virginia managed to pin down the British general, Sir William Cornwallis, at Yorktown in 1781.

In the meantime, France had decided that the American colonists just might win. They were helped considerably to this conclusion by the surrender of British Major General John Burgoyne's entire

Valley Forge — Generals Washington and Lafayette at Knox Artillery Camp, 1777 by John Ward Dunsmore. Washington is on the left.

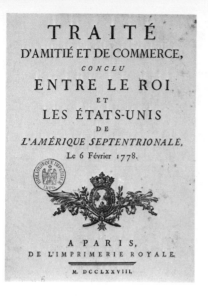

TRAITÉ
D'AMITIÉ ET DE COMMERCE,
CONCLU
ENTRE LE ROI
ET
LES ÉTATS-UNIS
DE
L'AMÉRIQUE SEPTENTRIONALE,
Le 6 Février 1778.

A PARIS,
DE L'IMPRIMERIE ROYALE.
M. DCCLXXVIII.

The title page of the Treaty of Alliance signed by France and pledging help to the United States during the Revolutionary War. The inscription reads as follows: "Treaty of friendship and commerce, concluded between the king and the United States of North America." The date is February 6, 1778.

army at Saratoga, New York. In 1778, France signed a formal Treaty of Alliance pledging, among other things, military support to the 13 states.

The 32,000 French sailors and 12,000 soldiers who served in America during the last years of the war were not immigrants. Many, of course, did stay, but most of them were military men assigned to duty in British North America, as well as the West Indies where France had possessions, such as Santo Domingo, which had to be protected from the British. When the war was over, they returned to France, but their presence in America added gaiety and color and, above all, hope in the fight for independence. More than hope — they tipped the scales, making it possible to win the war.

Louis of France had sent the flower of his army and they landed at Newport, Rhode Island, in 1780 with all the pageantry typical of the French. There were troopers in light blue jackets trimmed with yellow, breeches also of yellow, fur-trimmed capes and plumed caps. There were regiments clad in white coats with rose, black or green facings, and regiments in blue coats with bright yellow facings and cuffs.

What was even more important was that they were under the command of a veteran officer, Jean-Baptiste Donatier de Vimeur, Comte de Rochambeau, a quiet man very different from Lafayette but without much doubt the best general France could have sent, and a man who from the beginning had an instinctive feeling for the problems facing Washington. In a wonderfully generous gesture, he gave Washington half of his remaining military funds to finance their famous march south.

A third Frenchman whose contribution to the victory of the American states was fully as great as that of Lafayette and Rochambeau was Francois Joseph Paul, Comte de Grasse. Admiral de Grasse commanded the French fleet of 28 ships of the line which succeeded in cutting off any escape by Cornwallis from Yorktown. De Grasse fought the one truly decisive battle of the Revolutionary

The Siege of Yorktown (left). Rochambeau, Washington, and Lafayette stand in the entranceway to the tent. The Comte de Rochambeau (right), Commander-In-Chief of the 12,000 French troops which landed in America in 1780.

U.S. postage stamp commemorating the 150th anniversary of the surrender of the British general Cornwallis, at the Battle of Yorktown. Washington is flanked by his French allies, General Rochambeau and Admiral De Grasse. This victory ended the Revolutionary War.

War, at sea off Yorktown, and it is an irony of history, as well as a tribute to the help of the French, that not one American took part.

The siege at Yorktown shows how the Americans and the French worked together. Cornwallis, with his 7,000 men, controlled most of Virginia. He had dug in at Yorktown to await further orders. He was opposed by only a small force of patriots under Lafayette. Washington, in New York, saw that he could trap Cornwallis. He and Rochambeau marched their forces overland from New York to Virginia. Admiral de Grasse sailed his fleet from the French West Indies to Chesapeake Bay to cut off Cornwallis' escape by sea. There De Grasse met and scattered a British rescue fleet in the vital and decisive action of the war. The six years of bitter fighting were over. The British decided to sue for peace — an act made possible, in part, by a French admiral who seized control of the seas at the right moment and held it just long enough.

The presence of the French troops naturally had caused great excitement among the American patriots. The gallant French officers were entertained lavishly and the French found the American women charming. When the army sailed for home, there was universal regret. The qualities and characters of these French officers had done much to cement the friendship of the two countries.

Major Pierre Charles L'Enfant had come to fight for American independence. He settled here after the Revolutionary War was won.

Though they did not yet know it, the troops were sailing home to a France which soon would be torn apart by its own bloody revolution. Many of these men, sympathetic to the cause of liberty, equality and fraternity as they had seen it in America, would return to the new United States as political refugees — some to die there.

One of the men who stayed behind in America was Major Pierre Charles L'Enfant, an army engineer and an architect whose enthusiasm for the colonies' struggle had brought him to America in 1777. After the war, during which he fought and was wounded, he drew up the plan for the new capital city of Washington. That plan, in which the major avenues of the city extend out from Capitol Hill like the spokes of a wheel, is engraved upon the marker on his grave in Arlington cemetery in Washington. L'Enfant also supervised the remodeling of the old city hall on Wall Street in New York City for the use of the first federal congress.

The present New York City Hall, the work of the French engineer and architect, Joseph Francois Mangin. The architectural style is that of Louis XVI.

Joseph Francois Mangin, another French engineer and architect, designed and built the New York City Hall.

During the 1780s, before the outbreak of the French Revolution, a small but steady stream of Frenchmen migrated to the new United States, many of them with visions of creating a perfect society, a Utopia. The Scioto project in Ohio, is an example of the dreamy idealism with which some of the French approached life in America. A group of Frenchmen acquired some 10,000 acres and eventually 600 immigrants from France attempted to settle there. They soon found that their titles to the land were vague. The project fell apart, the immigrants moving on to other parts of the United States and today, the town of Gallipolis, Ohio, and its county of Gallia are the only reminders of the project.

2. *Royalist Refugees Flee the French Revolution*

But the time for dreamy-eyed idealism was about over. In France, during the 1790s, the Revolution was turning the old order upside down and thousands of French men and women were faced with the practical necessity of fleeing for their lives. At the same time, a revolution in Santo Domingo caused about nine-tenths of the white people living there to flee. The Creoles from Santo Domingo, who were people of Spanish and French descent, fled to the central and southern United States, while the refugees from France flocked into the northern sections of the country. How many came is difficult to determine now, but estimates range from 10,000 to 25,000.

For the next 60 years these political emigres, as they were called, were to come, driven out of France by one political upheaval after another. Not all were true immigrants. Many returned to France just as soon as it was safe to do so. But many stayed, enriching American life immeasurably and bringing to it the graces and culture of old France.

One of the most interesting things about the political emigres was the fact that most of them were either members of the nobility or aristocracy of France or persons who had served the French upper class. In addition to the noblemen and army officers who had fled for their lives, there were fencing and dancing masters, hairdressers, perfumers, barbers, clothing designers and cooks.

The last group stirred up a revolution of their own in American cookery, creating a love for French dishes and adding new words to the vocabularies of Americans: omelet, puree, mayonnaise, hors d'oeuvres, bouillon, consomme, saute, filet, julienne, a la king, au gratin, cafe au lait, canape.

They settled in the cities, chiefly New York, Philadelphia, Charleston and New Orleans, where their services would be in demand. Most of them established businesses and put down roots.

For many of the aristocrats, however, life in America was not a new adventure but an unfortunate exile from the land they loved. Unlike the Huguenots and the men of New France, they did not make farmers or even villagers and they were not used to toil. What they had been used to was a highly civilized and sophisticated life in the great cities of France, chiefly Paris. They tried to establish the salons they had known in Paris — the brilliant gatherings of witty, intelligent, cultured and often famous people, usually in the home of a lovely hostess — but life in America, on the edge of the frontier, just did not make this possible.

The aristocratic exiles, the army officers, the intellectuals who

were out of favor with the revolutionists at home, were not particularly happy in America. Equality, as it actually was practiced in
America, horrified many of them. Like other refugees from time
immemorial, they sold their jewels and other belongings in order
to live. Many of them also accepted, gallantly, gracefully and, rather
sadly, the necessity of working. They did what any civilized and
displaced Frenchman would do in such circumstances: they taught,
often at leading universities; they wrote; they played in orchestras;
they became chefs. Some of the military men, especially those who
had served in the American Revolution, received appointments from
President Washington. One became commander at West Point.

These refugees were a colorful and interesting group and included some of the most illustrious names in France. Louis
Phillippe, a member of the royal house of France who would one
day (1830 to 1848) be king of France himself, lived in New York,
Philadelphia, Kentucky and New Orleans. One writer "once attended a dinner given by Louis Phillippe at his modest lodgings
(in New York) where one half of the guests were seated upon the
side of the bed for want of room to place chairs elsewhere."

Tallyrand, the French statesman, lived in the United States for
three years. He later became foreign minister under Napoleon.

In Philadelphia, these and other aristocratic, brilliant but
poverty-stricken refugees mingled with the American statesmen
who were forming the new government. Philadelphia, as a result,
became the great center for the political emigres from France.
They could be found in other sections of Pennsylvania, too. A
party of exiles formed a French colony, known as Asylum, on the
banks of the Susquehanna River in 1794. It was planned by De
Noailles, Lafayette's brother-in-law, who also had fought in the
American Revolutionary War. The town existed for about 10 years
and had a small theater, a chapel, a bakery and typically French
shops clustered around the public square. One house always was

kept ready to receive King Louis XVI of France and his queen, Marie Antoinette, if they should escape to America.

Later, after the execution of the king and queen, the legend of the "Lost Dauphin" spread to America. The dauphin, the small son of Louis and Marie Antoinette, was the heir to the throne of France and actually was king in name only — as Louis XVII — for two years after the death of his father. Then the boy disappeared. Stories grew that he had managed to escape from prison, that he was in hiding in various countries, including the United States. For many years after the French Revolution, enterprising Frenchmen turned up in America claiming that they were the "Lost Dauphin." A cloud of mystery still surrounds the fate of this little boy — even though historians today are convinced that he died in 1795, at the age of 10, apparently while still in prison.

3. *Early French Contributions to American Industry and Commerce*

Not all the political emigres returned to France when the French Revolution ended. The Du Pont family was one outstanding example. Pierre Samuel Du Pont de Nemours was a publisher in Paris until the Jacobins, the militant leaders of the French Revolution, forced him to stop publication. He came to America in 1799 and settled near Wilmington, Delaware. Within five years the Du Ponts were manufacturing gun powder, helped in their new enterprise by Alexander Hamilton. President Thomas Jefferson gave government orders to Eleuthere Irenee Du Pont, Pierre's younger son.

The outbreak of the War of 1812 put the Du Pont family business on a solid foundation. After that came the millions of pounds of gun powder needed to blow up endless stumps as the people of an expanding United States cleared away forests to plant crops.

Today the company is the largest manufacturer of chemical products in the world. It still headquarters in Wilmington. Members of the Du Pont family have been naval officers, soldiers and diplomats. Henry Algernon du Pont was a United States senator from Delaware from 1906 to 1917.

Even prior to the Du Ponts, however, a young French Huguenot immigrant, only 18 years of age at the time, opened a business that has endured and flourished until today. The P. Lorillard Company, tobacco merchants and manufacturers, traces its origin back to a day in 1760 when Pierre Lorillard opened his tobacco shop in New York town, shortly after his arrival from Montbeliard, France.

Another remarkable man of this era was Stephen Girard, who helped save the United States treasury in 1811 and who also helped the new nation finance the War of 1812. A ship's captain from Bordeaux, France, Girard had come to the United States in 1776 and settled in Philadelphia. He made millions of dollars in foreign trade, real estate, insurance and banking, and he gave away much of it. Girard was interested in agriculture, too, and imported fruit trees from France which he loved to plant. A many-sided man, he helped refugees from France and during the epidemics of yellow fever, which broke out periodically, he gave all his time to nursing

This is just one of many of the Du Pont Company's large, modern plants. It is located at Waynesboro, Virginia, and makes orlon and other synthetic fibers. Company headquarters are still at Wilmington, Delaware, where the family settled after fleeing from the French Revolution.

Stephen Girard, a leading shipowner and merchant of the early 19th century.

the sick. He read widely, especially the works of the French philosophers, and named his ships for them — the *Voltaire*, the *Rousseau* the *Montesquieu*.

When Girard died in 1831, he left most of his huge fortune to found Girard College in Philadelphia "for educating poor white orphan boys," as his will said. His will also provided that the boys admitted to the college "shall be fed plain but wholesome food, clothed with plain and decent apparel (no distinctive dress ever to be worn) and lodged in a plain but safe manner."

4. *More Refugees — Royalist and Napoleonic*

For most of the 19th century — at least until about 1870 — political refugees fleeing from one form of French government or another continued to come to America. Charleston, South Carolina, received several hundred refugees from the revolution in Santo Domingo during the 1790s. Added to these were exiles from France. They established a French theater, attempted a French newspaper and argued politics warmly. They also were inclined to stay for good.

About 4,000 exiles went to New Orleans in 1791. They included the first company of actors in Louisiana. Almost 20 years later, 6,000 more came from Cuba. Orginally from Santo Domingo, these French refugees had been forced out of Cuba when Napoleon went to war with Spain.

The royalist refugees were followed, as French politics twisted and turned, by the Bonapartist exiles, especially generals and officers, who had served under Napoleon Bonaparte and were thereby accused of betraying the king. These were a colorful and distinguished group, too. They began coming to the United States in 1815. For awhile, there were exciting rumors that Napoleon, aided by Stephen Girard, had escaped from his guarded exile on the bleak island of St. Helena and had fled to America. Certainly his two brothers, Joseph and Jerome, came and Joseph acquired 150,000 acres of land in New York which was intended as a refuge for Napoleon. There seem to have been a number of rather vague plots for rescuing him. However, the former emperor ended his life rather unromantically, still in exile on St. Helena.

Jerome Bonaparte married an American, Elizabeth Patterson of Baltimore, Maryland. Although Jerome returned to Europe, their son, Jerome Napoleon Bonaparte, founded the American Bonaparte family and his son, Charles Joseph Bonaparte, was secretary of the treasury and attorney general under President Theodore Roosevelt.

Then there is the story of Demopolis, Alabama, a town which still exists, although its French origins have disappeared, for the most part. This settlement, and another at Aigleville, were launched with considerable fanfare. The French Agriculture and Manufacturing Society was formed to promote cultivation of the vine and olive and a land grant was obtained from Congress. In 1816, 140 settlers departed southward, with an assortment of plants to start off the project. At Mobile, Alabama, they were entertained at a

John James Audubon, America's great artist-naturalist and painter of the famous work *The Birds of America*. He was born in the French colony of Santo Domingo, which is now the country Haiti.

public dinner in their honor. Unfortunately, after the French had laid out the two sites, it developed that they lay outside their grant. But they built their towns anyway and installed in them their books, silks, ribbons, parasols and guitars. For a time, the village looked like a small French town, but the project failed. Many of the families moved away to New Orleans or to Texas where one colony of exiles was, for a time, under military discipline and the campaigns of Napoleon were refought on paper almost every day.

U. S. commemorative stamp, part of the Famous American Scientist series issued in 1940, which honored John James Audubon.

The John James Audubon commemorative stamp of 1963. It reproduces his engraving of the "Columbia Jay." The original print hangs in the National Gallery of Art, Washington, D.C.

By no means all of the French who came to America after the American Revolution were propelled here by political upheavals at home. The French came rather steadily, some from the West Indies, some from France. In 1804, John James Audubon, a nineteen-year-old who had been born in Santo Domingo, came to claim an estate near Philadelphia which his father, who had served in the Revolutionary War, had bought. Audubon became known as the United States' foremost naturalist and his pictures of birds, which were not only highly accurate but works of art as well, "introduced us," it has been said, "to the birds of America."

5. *French Life at the End of the 19th Century*

The French in America displayed an enthusiastic interest in affairs in old France, which were reported in the many French-language newspapers which sprang up. New York had at least four at one point. One was the *Courrier des Etats-Unis*, which had a long career. Philadelphia had three and Charleston at least two. Ten French newspapers flourished at one time in New Orleans. In addition, English-language newspapers carried some news stories and advertisements in French. New York, Philadelphia, New Orleans and Charleston were proud of their libraries of French volumes — Philadelphia had some 2,000 books. French was taught in academies and universities and by private tutors and the ability to speak French took on a certain social glamor. During the early 19th century, publishers did a brisk business turning out textbooks on the French language.

As the 19th century neared its end, the French newspapers and other publications began to die out, except in Louisiana. As America expanded westward and was, at the same time, flooded with great waves of immigrants from other countries, perhaps the opportunities for using the French language became increasingly limited and the French, themselves, were losing their identity as they became Americanized.

Wherever the French settled in large enough numbers, they formed colonies which showed great vigor. New York was an example. When news of the French Revolution of 1848 reached New York, the French there organized a great festival and staged an illumination of the city to celebrate what they felt was the return of the spirit of liberalism to the old country. Excitement was so great that whenever a ship from Europe docked in the harbor, people crowded the docks to wait for the latest dispatches.

In 1870-71, the French in New York — and elsewhere — followed the events of the Franco-Prussian War with feverish interest. At the end of the war, they helped refugees from Alsace-Lorraine, which had been returned to Germany, settle in America.

Most communities with any sizeable number of men and women of French ancestry annually celebrated Bastille Day, July 14, the French "Independence Day," and it still is celebrated each year in New Orleans. In 1889 the 100th anniversary of the fall of the Bastille was celebrated in French-American communities as far west as San Francisco, which held a three-day festival.

When the Civil War broke out, the French in many communities, North and South, organized companies and regiments. The

French in New York, pledging their support to the Union, organized a regiment of French volunteers. The Lafayette Guards went immediately into the war. They were a militia company made up entirely of men from New York who were of French ancestry. M. Le Baron Regis de Trobriand was colonel, a gentleman described by the newspapers as "well known in French literary circles as an able and accomplished writer." As uniforms, they wore blue overcoats and heavy duck pantaloons and the newspapers announced that "Madame Susand—a blooming young lady—accompanies the regiment as vivanderie (a seller of provisions); and an important fact to be mentioned is that M. Soyer is cook."

Wealthy Frenchmen largely filled the ranks of the 55th New York Volunteers. The Count of Paris, grandson of King Louis Phillippe and claimant to the throne of France, served briefly as a captain of volunteers in the Union army. General George B. McClellan praised him for bravery at the Battle of Gaines' Mill in 1862.

But the French from France were by no means the only Americans of French ancestry living in the United States. There were the French who had come from what is now Canada, and, to tell their story it is necessary to skip back a hundred years or more.

PART IV.

The Last 100 Years

1. *The Continuing Influence of the Early French*

During the last half of the 1700's, colonists living along the Atlantic coast began to spill across the Appalachian Mountains and onto the wide plains beyond. They found white men already living there, the descendants of the men who as explorers and fur traders had helped carve New France out of the wilderness. Except for the Indian tribes, these Frenchmen were the original settlers of the old Northwest Territory and of the Mississippi Valley.

When the territory east of the Mississippi was transferred from France to England in 1763, after the French and Indian War, these French men and women stayed behind in the settlements they had lived in for a generation — little French Catholic settlements such as Vincennes, in what is now Indiana; Kaskaskia in Illinois; St. Louis in Missouri, which was not yet part of the United States.

They clustered around a trading post or stockade, keeping alive their customs and language and living a carefree, easygoing existence. In the years just before the Civil War, people traveling through Indiana and Illinois would come upon these old French settlements. Their narrow lanes and galleried houses with low roofs had an Old World look. Each house would have a garden surrounded by a stone wall or fence. The people lived in the villages and farmed in the fields which surrounded the towns so that, in the European manner, the farmers would journey out from the villages each day. The fields usually were common lands — that is, used or owned by all the villagers. Center of village activity was the church with its adjoining convent and school.

Sometimes described as "indifferent farmers," these old French settlers were gay and fond of dancing to the music of their fiddles. They still traded in furs, especially in the northern states such as Minnesota and Wisconsin where a flourishing fur trading business lasted until the Civil War and did not completely die out, at least in Minnesota, until just before World War I.

2. *New Orleans and St. Louis*

The story of New Orleans, the "Paris of America," belongs to the story of these early settlers of New France because this fascinating city was founded by the French from Quebec in 1718 on the site of an old Indian camping ground. The early settlers lived on the Mississippi River front in a fortified square called the Vieux Carre — the "old square." It is now the famed French Quarter of the city and it has been carefully preserved. With its blend of old colonial French and Spanish architecture, the Vieux Carre has given the city much of its charm. The old quarter has been so little changed that even the names of the streets date from the earliest years of the colony. The streets are narrow and overhung with balconies of fine wrought iron in lacy patterns. They reflect New Orleans' varied past, for four different flags have flown over the city.

Until 1762, she was one of the most important cities of New France. At the end of the French and Indian War, France turned over to Spain New Orleans and the vast Louisiana Territory to keep it from falling to the British. In 1800, Napoleon Bonaparte forced Spain to return the territory to France and in 1803 he sold it to the United States in the great real estate transaction known as the Louisiana Purchase. During the War Between the States, New Orleans was a major port for the South. Hence, four flags — French, Spanish, American and the Stars and Bars of the Confederacy.

During the years of revolution after 1790, thousands of refugees from France, Spain and their West Indies possessions found their way to New Orleans, and great numbers of them settled down permanently. This gave the city its quaint mixture of French and Spanish and the people who were a combination of the two nationalities, the Creoles. New Orleans has become famous for its Creole cooking.

The unhappy story of the Acadians is part of the history of Louisiana, partly because of Longfellow's romantic poem, *Evangeline*. The Acadians were men and women of French blood who lived in Nova Scotia. After the British took over Nova Scotia, sometimes called Acadia, they decided it was necessary to deport all Acadians who refused to take the oath of allegiance to the British king. In 1755, about 6,000 men, women and children were ordered to leave the country. Some went to Massachusetts and other colonies, where they were met with much resentment.

Most, however, made the long hard journey south to New Orleans where today their descendants are the "Cajuns" of Louisiana. They have retained many of the old customs of 18th century France and they speak their own version of the French language. Originally, it was the dialect spoken in Normandy, in northern France, but English and Creole words have been mixed in with the French. Today there are hundreds of thousands of "Cajuns" in Louisiana.

Between 1800 and 1825, New Orleans was the center of culture of the Old South. The first permanent opera company in the United States was established in New Orleans before 1800 and, until after the Civil War, the city was the most important operatic center in America. In a space of just five years, 70 operas were performed in the New Orleans Theatre of St. Pierre. Writers flourished, too, and they produced novels, poetry and historical works.

The system of laws was very different from those used elsewhere in the United States where English common law was the basis for the legal system. New Orleans and Louisiana used the Code Napoleon, a collection of laws drawn together by Napoleon Bonaparte and based in part on old Roman laws and customs.

Even Christmas was different in New Orleans. Following the custom of Old France, Papa Noel, rather than Santa Claus, brought small gifts to the children on Christmas eve. The evening was spent gaily by the adults who sang and played games until it was time for midnight Mass at the church. New Year's Day, instead of Christmas, was the day of lavish gift-giving, accompanied by much feasting and celebrating of the new year.

In other ways, the traditions of France were transplanted to New Orleans. There were French dancing masters to teach the children of the more prosperous families. In the French convent schools, the gentle manners of Old France were taught. Families whose ancestors could be traced back to the years of Louis XIV lived in the grand manner, with plantations along the Mississippi and houses in New Orleans. They danced, they gambled, and they settled their arguments with duels fought out according to a strict code of honor, and they produced some colorful men.

One was Jean Laffite, who has been described as a smuggler, a pirate and a privateer—that is, the owner of an armed ship commissioned to attack the shipping of an enemy nation. During the War of 1812, Laffite was offered $30,000 by the British to help them in their attack on New Orleans. He refused it and instead offered his services to Andrew Jackson, the American commander. Laffite fought in the successful defense of the city and, in 1815, received a Presidential pardon for his past crimes.

The Louisiana Purchase turned over to the United States the vast lands stretching from the Mississippi to the Rocky Mountains and the Gulf of Mexico to what is now the Canadian border. It also brought under the American flag more small French settlements, established many years earlier, during the era of New France. One was St. Louis, now one of the great cities of the Mississippi but in 1800 a village of 669 persons — and 1,350 French books on science, medicine, engineering and philosophy.

Charles Dickens visited St. Louis in 1842 and described the town's French quarter and its quaint, picturesque houses and narrow, crooked street. The houses, he wrote, were "built of wood with tumble down galleries between the windows . . .

"Some of these ancient habitations, with high gable garret windows perking into the roofs, have a kind of French shrug about them; and being lopsided with age, appear to hold their heads askew besides, as if they were grimacing in astonishment at the American improvements."

3. *French Contributions in the 19th Century*

One of St. Louis' important men was Dr. Antoine Francois Saugrain de Vigni, an heroic old Indian fighter who was a physician, chemist and philosopher. He administered the first smallpox vaccine there in 1809.

At about the same time, near New Orleans, Dr. Francois Marie Prevost, a humble pioneer and surgeon, was performing successful Caesarean operations on slave women. Operating with no anesthetics, with crude instruments and no way of sterilizing them, Dr. Prevost saved lives at a time when doctors in New York and Europe were losing both mother and baby in this type of operation.

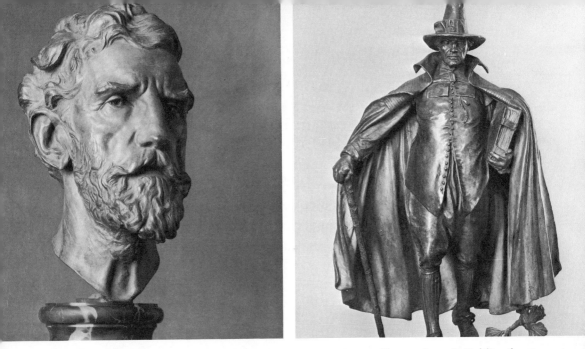

Augustus Saint-Gaudens *(left)*, one of America's great sculptors. He was born in Dublin, the son of a French shoemaker and an Irish mother. This head is by John Flanagan, a prominent 20th century sculptor. Saint-Gaudens' statuette *The Puritan (right)* was completed in 1898. It is now in the Metropolitan Museum of Art, New York.

The memorial to Rear Admiral David G. Farragut *(left)* the man who said, "Damn the torpedoes. Full speed ahead!" was sculptured by Saint-Gaudens. The statue stands in a square in New York City. Farragut was a naval hero of the Civil War and took New Orleans from the Confederates. The Saint-Gaudens sculpture of William Tecumseh Sherman *(right)*, the Union general who led the famous march from Atlanta, Georgia, to the sea, is also in New York.

Other names of French-Americans who were important during the 19th century crowd in here. In 1848, Bernard Saint-Gaudens, a French shoemaker, and his Irish wife came to America with their baby, Augustus, who had been born in Dublin. When he grew up, Augustus Saint-Gaudens decided to be an artist. He served first as apprentice to a stone-cameo cutter. Later he studied in Paris and Rome and eventually became one of the world's great sculptors. One of his greatest works is the statue portraying grief which is on the grave of Mrs. Henry Adams in Washington, D.C. He also created a number of monuments honoring American heroes, and the famous statuette *The Puritan*.

The Reverend William Passevant who founded hospitals in Chicago, Pittsburgh, and Milwaukee.

Dr. Edward Trudeau, a pioneer in the battle against tuberculosis.

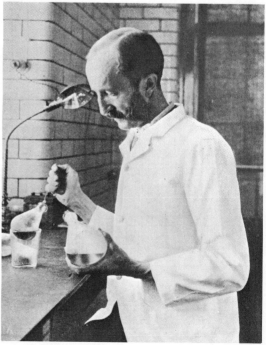

Octave Chanute was born in Paris and came to America in 1838 as a child. He became a leading civil engineer, building bridges and railroads. Then he literally took to the air. He became interested in aerodynamics. By the 1890s he had developed gliders which he launched on short flights from the sand dunes along the shores of Lake Michigan. The Wright brothers felt he was one of the great pioneers in this field. He invented the Chanute bi-plane which was a forerunner of the Wrights' first glider.

There was Jean Baptist Julien, who opened a small restaurant in Boston and became famous for his "consomme Julien." There was the Reverend William Passevant who founded hospitals in Chicago, Pittsburgh and Milwaukee, and Dr. Edward Trudeau who was a pioneer in the battle against tuberculosis. He founded a sanitarium for tuberculosis patients—the first of its kind in the world—at Saranac Lake, New York, and later established the Saranac Laboratory, the first in America for the study of the disease.

Henry David Thoreau, the New England naturalist, philosopher and writer, was of Scottish and French descent. There were the poets Philip Freneau and Sidney Lanier. Henry Wadsworth Longfellow was a descendant of John Alden and his French Huguenot bride, Priscilla Mullins or Molines, about whom Longfellow wrote in *The Courtship of Miles Standish.*

And there was Professor Edouard de Laboulaye, a French-American who felt something should be done to commemorate the alliance between France and America which had begun during the American Revolution. The result of his proposal was the creation of the Statue of Liberty, the largest statue ever made. It was designed by the French sculptor, Frederic Auguste Bartholdi, presented to the American people in 1884, and erected on Bedloe's Island in New York harbor, where in the 1650s Isaac Bedloe had pastured his cows.

The Statue of Liberty, presented to the American people by France in 1884. It stands on an island in New York harbor where Isaac Bedloe, a French Huguenot, once pastured his cows.

4. The French-Canadians

One important group which must be mentioned is the French-Canadians, who came to the United States after the Civil War. They were the descendants of those Frenchmen who came to Quebec in the 1600s. Proud of their ancient culture, they spoke a form of French and lived according to customs which dated back to the days of Louis XIV, mixed in with changes which had taken place during their long years in North America.

About 100 years or so ago, the French-Canadians began moving down from Canada into the Great Lakes region and the states along the Canadian boundary. Many were fur traders, colorful voyageurs, and they settled down as pioneers in a new land. One group helped found the city of St. Paul, Minnesota.

It was to New England, however, that most of the French-Canadians went. By the 1870s, French-Canadians moving into the New England states unfortunately ran into trouble.

They came to escape the poverty of their farms in Quebec and to earn some money in the mills and factories, and they came by the thousands — 275,000 by 1900. They were obedient workers, willing to labor long hours for low wages, and to put their children to work, too, in violation of the laws regarding sending children to school. They cared little about joining American trade unions. Considering everything, New England mill owners thought they were such desirable workers that they sent agents into the villages of Quebec to recruit them.

In New England, the French-Canadians and that other large group of immigrants, the Irish, naturally collided head-on. The French were pushing the Irish out of their jobs. But there was another problem. The Catholic church in Quebec was fast losing its people to New England. Unable to stem the flow across the border, the church decided to send its priests with them and the result was another head-on collision. The Irish, who had dominated the church and the priesthood in New England for some years, resented this intrusion, too. Feelings became so heated that the battle actually was carried all the way to Rome.

In time, though, tempers cooled and many French Catholic churches and parochial schools were set up in the heart of the land of the Puritans. Eventually, the French-Canadians began to blend into American life. Most of the New England states had French-Canadians in their legislatures and at least one served as governor of Massachusetts. Some cities had such a large number of the French that both English and French were spoken as a matter of course.

For the French-Canadian, life revolved about the family circle. Next in importance came his church and then the parochial school where the French language and customs were kept alive. As these Frenchmen from Canada came to be accepted, their fine qualities were recognized — loyalty to family, church and language, ruggedness, generosity, warmheartedness and frugality.

5. *Summing-Up French Immigration*

Accurate figures on immigration to the United States were not kept until passage of the Act of 1819. This required the captain of all vessels arriving from abroad to deliver a list of passengers according to age, sex, occupation and "country to which they severally belonged." At first, only arrivals at ports on the Atlantic Ocean or the Gulf of Mexico were listed. By 1850, arrivals at Pacific ports were included.

In 1820, 371 French immigrants were listed as having arrived in the United States. After that, the figures multiply with each decade: 8,479 from 1821 to 1830; 45,575 from 1831 to 1840; 77,262 from 1841 to 1850. This, however, was a period of very heavy emigration from Europe. The number of French who came to this country should be compared with such figures as the 434,626 emigrants from Germany or the 780,719 from Ireland during the decade between 1841 and 1850.

French immigration has always been small but steady. In the years between 1820 and 1964, a total of 703,789 French immigrants came to the United States, according to the records of the Immigration and Nationalization Service. This means an average of slightly less than 5,000 French immigrants each year.

Immigration from France

1821-1830	371	1911-1920	61,897
1821-1830	8,497	1921-1930	49,610
1831-1840	45,575	1931-1940	12,623
1841-1850	77,262	1941-1950	38,809
1851-1860	76,358	1951-1960	51,121
1861-1870	35,986	1961	4,403
1871-1880	72,206	1962	3,931
1881-1890	50,464	1963	4,926
1891-1900	30,770	1964	5,598
1901-1910	73,379		

6. *The French Influence Upon America*

The influence of France upon American life and culture is almost beyond measure. The great French philosophers, such as Voltaire and Rousseau who believed in the equality of man, were read by many of the leaders of Colonial America who helped shape the new nation. Years later, American artists went to Paris to study under the great French painters and sculptors. Still later, after World War I, a group of American expatriate writers, such as Ernest Hemingway and F. Scott Fitzgerald, went to Paris, where they produced work which has profoundly influenced American literature.

The French always have greatly influenced American manners, fashions and cooking. During the early 1800s, taverns and inns began to be called hotels, cooks and bakers became chefs and their eating places were renamed restaurants. French immigrants introduced breads made with yeast, omelettes, and artichokes.

Pierre ("Poppa") Laffitte was a famous French chef who came to the United States in 1889. He worked for a New York restaurant until 1915 when he opened his own Restaurant Laffitte which he ran in the classic French tradition.

Large numbers of immigrants from France who have come to the United States in the last 75 years have been teachers—college and university professors, tutors, private school and high school teachers. Many, like Laffitte, also became cooks or chefs, of course; others, domestic servants. Until about 1940, there was a great demand on the part of wealthy Americans for French chauffeurs, governesses and "ladies' maids." But World War II, which brought better paying jobs in vital war industries, drew most people away from domestic service.

The French also transplanted the industries of France to the United States. They became fashion designers, clothing manufacturers. They went into the perfume and cosmetic business. The names of French-Americans are found in almost all phases of American life, ranging from the arts to the military to science to industry.

The LaFollette family of Wisconsin has produced some of the most famous political figures of French ancestry in modern times. Robert LaFollette, Sr., served his state as governor, congressman and senator until his death in 1925. Robert, Jr., was named senator

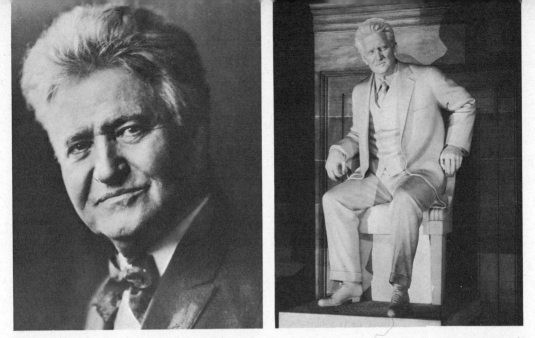

Robert Marion La Follette, Sr. *(left)*, of Wisconsin, known as "Fighting Bob." He was elected governor three times and then senator three times. In 1924 he ran for President on the Progressive Party ticket. He was elected to the Senate Hall of Fame. His statue *(right)* stands in Statuary Hall, the National Capitol, Washington, D. C.

"Fighting Bob's" son, Robert M. La Follette, Jr. *(left)*, was elected senator from Wisconsin upon his father's death. He was re-elected to three more terms, but was defeated in the election of 1946. Philip Fox La Follette *(right)*, the second son of "Fighting Bob," served two terms as governor of Wisconsin during the 1930's.

on his father's death, and then elected to three more terms. Philip, a younger son, was governor of Wisconsin. Bronson LaFollette, son of Robert LaFollette, Jr., is attorney general of Wisconsin.

Two Nobel prize winners have been Americans born in France. Dr. Alexis Carrel was a surgeon and biologist who was awarded the Nobel prize in 1915 for his research in stitching, or suturing, blood vessels. He later experimented with developing a mechanical heart.

Dr. Andre F. Cournand, a physiologist who is professor of medicine in the College of Physicians and Surgeons, Columbia University, New York, was awarded the Nobel prize in medicine and physiology in 1956, Dr. Cournand is the holder of many other awards, including the Lasker award from the United States Public Health Service. He served with the French army in World War I and was decorated with the Croix de Guerre.

Edward L. Cournand, who was born in Paris in 1897 and edu-

Dr. Alexis Carrel, the first French-born American to receive the Nobel prize. He was given the 1912 award in medicine for his research on the suturing of blood vessels.

Dr. Andre F. Cournand was awarded the Nobel prize in medicine and physiology in 1956. He is professor of medicine at the College of Physicians and Surgeons, Columbia University, New York City.

cated at the Sorbonne, now lives in New York where he is president and director of Lanvin-Parfums, Inc.

A list of renowned scientists would include the name of John Lawrence LeConte, one of America's foremost entomologists and a descendant of a long line of scientists who were of Huguenot stock.

In literature and the arts there is the Benet family: Stephen Vincent Benet who won the Pulitzer prize in 1929 for his epic poem, *John Brown's Body;* his brother, William Rose Benet, also a poet and Pulitzer prize winner in 1942 for *The Dust Which is God,* a novel in verse; and their sister, Laura Benet, poet and author of books for young people.

There was Charles Macomb Flandrau, author of *Viva Mexico!,* who was the son of a hero of the bloody Sioux War in Minnesota. Novelist John P. Marquand also was of French ancestry. Will Durant, historian, philosopher and author of the monumental series of books, *The Story of Civilization,* is a French-Canadian.

John La Farge was one of America's most talented and versatile painters and has been called the "father of mural painting in America." Oliver La Farge is a writer deeply interested in the

Novelist John P. Marquand, winner of the 1937 Pulitzer prize for his novel *The Late George Apley,* is one of many distinguished American literary figures of French ancestry.

American Indians. He was awarded the Pulitzer prize in 1929 for his first novel, *Laughing Boy*. His father, Christopher La Farge, was a well-known architect.

In music, there is singer Lily Pons, composer Darius Milhaud and the late conductor of the San Francisco Symphony Orchestra, Pierre Monteux. Claudette Colbert and Charles Boyer are among many French names in the entertainment world.

In 1929, John C. Garand, a government designer, invented the rifle which became the official rifle of the United States army and Marine Corps and did such deadly service during World War II. Allen Du Mont worked out many of the basic inventions which made possible the development of radar and television and Raymond Loewy won fame as an industrial designer. In the fashion world there are Lilly Dache, famous as a hat designer, and Pauline Trigere, the dress designer, and her brother and partner, Robert.

Pierre Monteux, for many years conductor of the San Francisco Symphony Orchestra, was born in Paris. He came to America about 1917.

Claudette Colbert has been active in the theatre and motion pictures since 1924. She was born in Paris and brought to the United States in 1910. Her real name was Lily Chauchoin.

Charles Boyer was born in Figeac, France, in 1899. He made his acting debut in Paris, and has since starred in many roles. He has also served as president of the French Research Foundation, and has been active in the American Friends of France and French War Relief.

John C. Garand, inventor of the U.S. Army's semi-automatic rifle.

Admiral George Dewey, commander of America's Asiatic squadron during the Spanish-American War. He won the Battle of Manila Bay against the Spanish fleet.

Brigidier General (retired) James P. S. Devereux was a major in the marine corps during the early weeks of World War II and fought in the defense of Wake Island.

The Garand rifle. From 1936 until the early 1960's, this gun was the official rifle of the United States army and marine corps.

In the armed forces there have been such men as Admiral George Dewey, the hero of the Spanish-American War. Lieutenant General Leonard T. Gerow and Major James P. S. Devereux, the defender of Wake Island during the early weeks of World War II, are contemporary military leaders of French ancestry.

Robert G. LeTourneau devised the great earth-moving machines which have made it possible for the United States to build huge airstrips and super-highways. He is the world's largest manufacturer of earth-moving equipment. Of Huguenot stock, he

Lieutenant General Leonard T. Gerow commanded the U.S. Fifth Army Corps in Europe during World War II. His decorations include the Distinguished Service Medal, the Legion of Honor, and the French Croix de Guerre.

Robert G. LeTourneau heads the LeTourneau Company, the world's largest manufacturer of earth-moving equipment. He devised the huge machines which have literally changed the face of the earth.

also is a well-known lay Christian evangelist who thinks of himself as "God's partner" in all phases of his life.

At least four American colleges and universities either have been founded or heavily endowed by the French in America. They are Girard College in Philadelphia; Tulane University in New Orleans; Vassar College in Poughkeepsie, New York, and the Julliard Musical Foundation in New York City.

Four American presidents were of French descent: John Tyler, James Garfield, Theodore Roosevelt and Franklin Delano Roosevelt. Franklin Roosevelt could rightfully claim to be a true American because he also was part-English, part-Scottish, part-Dutch and part-Swedish. However, his mother is from the Delano family

Sarah Delano Roosevelt and her son Franklin Delano Roosevelt. President Roosevelt held office longer than any other man—from 1933 to 1945. His mother's name was originally De La Noye. She was a descendant of Phillippe de La Noye, a Huguenot who came to America in 1621.

which traces its beginnings in America to a Huguenot named Phillippe de La Noye who came to American in 1621 on the ship *Fortune* and settled at Plymouth with the Pilgrims.

Perhaps nowhere in America can the contribution of the French be seen more clearly than in the person of President John F. Kennedy's First Lady, Jacqueline Bouvier Kennedy. During her three years in the White House, Mrs. Kennedy, a descendant of an old French family which settled in New York, undertook to recapture some of the historical flavor of the most important home in the country and to restore or put back into use lovely old furnishings which had been stored away.

In doing so, Mrs. Kennedy helped to underline once again France's historic influence on America. The early presidents, particularly, turned to France for the artistic touches which would help soften life in the raw capital city. Jefferson had a French chef and was roundly critized by Patrick Henry for "abjuring his native vituals." Jefferson, James Madison, James Monroe, Andrew Jackson and James Knox Polk all ordered furniture, table services, silverware and other furnishings, such as candelabra, from France.

Today it is possible to see in this historic mansion, pieces from the magnificent silver service ordered by Jackson and made by Martin Biennais, a leading French goldsmith.

In the Red Room is a card table and in the ground floor hall a small pier table, both made by Charles Honore Lannuier of Paris. In the Blue Room is a pier table and three chairs made by Pierre-Antoine Bellange of Paris, ordered especially for that room by President Monroe. Monroe had to refurnish the burned-out White House after the War of 1812.

The official home of the American Presidents symbolizes the contribution of French culture to America and those many thousands of French-Americans, living and dead, who have given so much to their adopted country.

Jacqueline Bouvier Kennedy with her husband, the late President John F. Kennedy, and President de Gaulle of France, at the Paris Opera. As First Lady of the United States Mrs. Kennedy sought to restore to the White House some of the historic furnishings originally obtained from France.

ACKNOWLEDGEMENTS

The illustrations are reproduced through the courtesy of: pp. 6, 15 (top), 18, Minnesota Historical Society; pp. 9, 53, 56, 57, French Embassy Press and Information Division; pp. 11, 15 (bottom left), 35, 42, 47, 49, 59, 68 (top), 85 (top right), Library of Congress; pp. 13, 85 (top left and bottom), State Historical Society of Wisconsin; p. 15 (bottom right), Ludington Chamber of Commerce; pp. 16, 20, 25, 30, 37, 54, 58, 68 (bottom), 69, Post Office Department, Division of Philately; p. 17, the Singer Company; p. 19, University of Minnesota, Duluth, Photo Service; p. 21, Michigan Bell Telephone Company; p. 22, Public Archives of Canada; pp. 29, 40, 55 (top), The Smithsonian Institution, Division of Numismatics; p. 36, Bowdoin College Museum of Art; p. 38, New England Mutual Life Insurance Company, Boston; p. 50, National Gallery of Art; p. 55 (bottom), Sons of the Revolution in the State of New York, Headquarters, Fraunces Tavern, New York City; p. 60, Art Commission, City of New York; p. 64, E. I. du Pont de Nemours & Co.; p. 77 (top left and right), the Metropolitan Museum of Art; p. 78 (left), Passavant Hospital, Chicago; p. 78 (right), National Tuberculous Association; p. 80, U.S. Department of the Interior; p. 86 (left), Rockefeller Foundation; p. 86 (right), Columbia University; p. 87, Dorothy Wilding; p. 88 (left), San Francisco Symphony Orchestra; p. 88 (right), station KSTP, Minneapolis; p. 89 (top left), Station WCCO, Minneapolis; p. 89 (top right), 90 (bottom left), U.S. Army; p. 89 (bottom left), The National Archives; p. 89 (bottom right), U.S. Marine Corps; p. 90 (top), The Smithsonian Institution, U.S. National Museum; p. 90 (bottom right), Le Tourneau Co.; p. 91, Wide World Photos, Inc.

ABOUT THE AUTHOR...

Virginia Brainard Kunz is a native Minnesotan whose roots reach deep into America's past. Her first American forebear, Daniel Brainard, came to Massachusetts from England in 1649 and married a descendant of the Pilgrims who were on the *Mayflower*. Later Brainards went west, and Mrs. Kunz's great-grandfather Oliver Brainard II arrived in Minnesota in 1866. On the maternal side, her great-grandfather was born in Norway and immigrated to Minnesota. Her grandfather married into a French-Canadian family that immigrated to Quebec in 1690. The grandfather of Mrs. Kunz's husband came to the United States from Germany in the 1860's. She, herself, graduated in 1943 from Iowa State University, and embarked upon a journalism career with the Minneapolis newspapers the *Star* and the *Tribune*. At present she is Executive Secretary of the Ramsey County Historical Society and editor of the journal, *Ramsey County History*. She is also a free lance writer, and author of *Muskets to Missiles: A Military History of Minnesota*. She is listed in *Who's Who of American Women, Who's Who in the Midwest* and *Who's Who in Minnesota*. Mrs. Kunz, her husband, and their two children, reside in Minneapolis.

The IN AMERICA *Series*

The ENGLISH *in America*
The FRENCH *in America*
The GERMANS *in America*
The IRISH *in America*
The ITALIANS *in America*
The NEGRO *in America*
The SCOTS *and* SCOTCH-IRISH *in America*
The SWEDES *in America*

Additional titles will be added regularly. For a complete
list of all our books please write:

 LERNER PUBLICATIONS COMPANY
133 First Avenue North, Minneapolis, Minnesota 55401